Kid-Jitsu®

Teaching Children the Art of Brazilian Jiu-Jitsu

Instructor's Manual

Larry Shealy

With Technical Advisor
Charles Dos Anjos

Outskirts Press, Inc.
Denver, Colorado

Kid-Jitsu
Instructor's Manual
Teaching Children the Art of Brazilian Jiu-Jitsu
All Rights Reserved
Copyright © 2006 Larry Shealy
Cover Image © 2006 Larry Shealy
All Rights Reserved. Used With Permission.

Outskirts Press
http://www.outskirtspress.com

ISBN-10: 1-59800-944-3
ISBN-13: 978-1-59800-944-6

Outskirts Press and the "OP" logo are trademarks belonging to
Outskirts Press, Inc.

Printed in the United States of America

Dedication

This manual is dedicated to my Instructor Master Royce Gracie and his father Grandmaster Helio Gracie. Helio Gracie took the jiu-jitsu that he and his brothers learned from the Japanese and modified the art to a point where proper leverage and technique would allow the "average" person to defeat bigger and stronger opponents in self-defense and fighting situations. This was the birth of Gracie Jiu-Jitsu and what is also commonly known as Brazilian Jiu-Jitsu.

Royce Gracie has made Brazilian Jiu-Jitsu a household word around the world with his early victories in the Ultimate Fighting Championships. At 6'1" and 175 pounds, the slight of build Gracie took on all comers from all martial arts "styles" and proved to the world the effectiveness of his father, Helios' style of Jiu-Jitsu.

Thank you, Grand Master Helio Gracie and Master Royce Gracie for sharing your family art with me and the rest of the world. I hope that the information contained herein will assist in passing your self-defense and fighting system, the techniques you created and your vision on to Karate and other martial arts schools and instructors all over the world. My true hope and desire is that these instructors will instill a solid foundation of Brazilian Jiu-Jitsu into all of the children that train in their various martial arts programs.

I also wish to dedicate this book to my students in my "original" "Kid-Jitsu®" classes and for giving "Mr. Larry" the idea and desire to make this book available to children and their Martial Arts Instructors all over the world. You guys and girls are the greatest! You know who you are.

Larry Shealy
Founder of "Kid-Jitsu®"

Product Liability Disclaimer

Read Before Use

This book's techniques are to be taught only for the use in lawful self-defense. These techniques can be dangerous, and must be taught and practiced responsibly, slowly, with great caution and with the appropriate protective gear.

This book is presented only as a means of preserving a unique aspect of the heritage of the martial arts. Neither the publisher nor the author make any representation, warranty or guarantee that the techniques described or illustrated in this book will be safe or effective in any specific self-defense situation or otherwise. You may be injured if you apply or train in the techniques illustrated in this book and neither the publisher nor the author is responsible for any such injury that may result. It is essential that you consult a physician regarding whether or not to attempt any technique described in this book. Specific self-defense responses illustrated in this book may not be justified in any particular situation in view of all of the circumstances or under applicable federal, state, or local law. Neither the publisher nor the author makes any representation or warranty regarding the legality or appropriateness of any technique mentioned in this book.

Foreword

"Larry Shealy has trained under Master Royce Gracie for many years and I have personally witnessed his commitment and progress for the last four years. Larry is a wonderful teacher, athlete and coach. Children will have great fun and develop as athletes and responsible people in his Licensed "Kid-Jitsu®" program. Parents will be very proud of what their children learn they can do with hard work, sportsmanship and team spirit."

"Kid-Jitsu®" will be a welcome and lucrative compliment to any martial arts curriculum out there in today's competitive marketplace." With his **"teaching the teacher how to teach"** *program you can easily implement Kid-Jitsu® into your already successful martial arts school." I am proud to be the technical advisor on this program for the children.*

-Charles Dos Anjos, Royce Gracie Black Belt
Sarasota, Florida

Larry Shealy is a pioneer in bringing Brazilian Jiu-Jitsu to the kids. His "Kid-Jitsu® program seamlessly pairs critical life-values that every parent would want their kids to know with techniques from one of the most effective martial arts available. A parent would be hard-pressed to find an instructor more committed to children and to their development as young people and martial artists.

-David Zavarella, M.B.A.
Royce Gracie Blue Belt Brazilian Jiu-Jitsu

Larry Shealy is a deeply devoted and expert instructor of "Kid-Jitsu®": Brazilian Jiu-Jitsu for Children. The mental and physical development "Kid-Jitsu® effects in each child who participates in this patented program is unparalleled. "Kid-Jitsu® teaches discipline, honor, and self-worth better than any program I have seen in practice today. His "Kid-Jitsu®" values program confirms the teachings that we, as parents, try to pass along to our children everyday. This curriculum of values combined with the physical art of Brazilian Jiu-Jitsu is a no-fail system.

-James Gibson, US Navy
Royce Gracie Blue Belt Brazilian Jiu-Jitsu,
Father of four children currently enrolled in "Kid-Jitsu®"

About the Kid-Jitsu Authors

Larry Shealy and Charles Dos Anjos: August 2006

Kid-Jitsu® Founder and Instructor:

Larry Shealy, M.B.A.

Larry Shealy began studying Gracie Brazilian Jiu-Jitsu in 1995 at the Gracie Jiu-Jitsu Academy in Torrance, California. He is a Black Belt in TKD and is also a 4-stripe Purple Belt under the direction and instruction of Master Royce Gracie. Larry is also a Certified Assistant Instructor in the Royce Gracie Jiu-Jitsu System and is the Royce Gracie Network Representative in Jacksonville, FL.

He has also learned Brazilian Jiu-Jitsu technique over the years from Rorion Gracie, Rickson Gracie, Royler Gracie, Rolker Gracie, Relson Gracie, Rodrigo Gracie, Carlos "Caique" Elias, Jacare' Cavalcante, Charles Dos Anjos, Steve Hall and Aparacido Bill. He has traveled extensively in the United States to study Brazilian Jiu-Jitsu and also two times to Rio de Janiero, Brazil to further his Brazilian Jiu-Jitsu studies. He has trained at the world famous Brazilian Jiu-Jitsu academies: The Gracie Jiu-Jitsu Academy in Torrance, California (Rorion and Royce Gracie), Gracie Barra in Barra de Tijuca, Rio de Janiero, Brazil with Carlos Gracie Jr. and Marcio Feitosa and Gracie Humatai in Rio de Janiero Brazil with Royler and Rolker Gracie.

In 2003, Larry began developing the "Kid-Jitsu®" program along with the "Kid-Jitsu® Values Program". This trademark registered program teaches children the fundamentals of Gracie Jiu-Jitsu, while weaving targeted values into each lesson within the "Kid-Jitsu®" Children's Curriculum.

His career has been quite varied with a Marketing Degree from Florida State University, a Masters Degree in Business from Jacksonville

University and over 20 successful years in Sales, Sales Training, and Sales Management in the Medical Device Field.

Larry received a black belt in TKD in the mid-1990's and had the good fortune of being <u>given</u> a ticket for admission to a **Rickson Gracie** seminar in Jacksonville, Florida. What he learned in a 2-day seminar was the catalyst for making not only an immediate change in his martial arts disciplines, but also a long-term change in his lifestyle and eventually his career.

Royce Gracie on a visit to JaxBJJ a Royce Gracie Network Affiliate,

in June 2006 with Larry Shealy

During this same time frame in the mid-1990's Larry was at the height of his success in the Medical Device Sales Industry and he spent a significant amount of time in California where he began training at the Gracie Academy in Torrance. It was also around this time that a rather strange and unique event began appearing on Pay-Per-View: The

Ultimate Fighting Challenge. (Later the name was changed to the Ultimate Fighting Championship). It was at this time that Larry, like many others, observed a skinny Brazilian kid beat all comers in 3-4 no holds barred, bare fisted fights in a given night.

Of course that skinny kid was Royce Gracie, and along with his family-style of Gracie Jiu-Jitsu he single handedly changed the way fighting would be done forever. Gracie Jiu-Jitsu became a household name and the fight game was changed forever; and so was Larry's life.
For Larry, Brazilian Jiu-Jitsu has morphed from a hobby and a means to stay in shape, to a total way of life. Along with the Black Belt in TKD and 4-stripe purple belt in Gracie Jiu-Jitsu, Larry Shealy is a Certified Instructor in the Haganah F.I.G.H.T. System under the leadership of Haganah Founder, Mike Lee Kanarek. He is also a Certified Instructor in Muay-Thai under world renowned Master Toddy out of Las Vegas, NV.

He teaches and trains in Brazilian Jiu-Jitsu and Kid-Jitsu® 6 days per week, personally teaching over 20 classes in a given week. He trains and spars with the young adult Brazilian Jiu-Jitsu students several times per week. He also teaches Haganah F.I.G.H.T. and Muay Thai classes throughout the week. He has over 200 students in his school ranging in age from 4 years old to 60 years of age.

His students say that he has a big heart, is a master motivator, is extremely loyal and has the God given ability to draw out the best in each student, young and old, that he comes in contact with.

The most ironic thing about the phenomenal growth in Larry's school is that this all has been accomplished in just **over one year as a full time business!!!** You too can have this type of growth, and beyond, as you implement "Kid-Jitsu®" into your martial arts curriculum.

Charles Dos Anjos:

Kid-Jitsu® Instructor and Technical Advisor:
Charles Dos Anjos

Charles Dos Anjos is a native Brazilian. Charles is from Recife, Brazil and is a very accomplished martial artist. Charles is a 1st Degree Black Belt in

Brazilian Jiu-Jitsu and is the Royce Gracie Jiu-Jitsu Network Representative in Sarasota, Florida.

Charles is an accomplished Brazilian Jiu-Jitsu competitor in Brazil where he won State Championships in his weight class six (6) times and in the Absolute Division six (6) times. He was the Regional Champion in Brazil on two occasions. In addition to his impressive Brazilian Jiu-Jitsu resume', Charles holds Black Belts in Judo, and Shotokon Karate.

Charles has collaborated with Larry Shealy in bringing "Kid-Jitsu® to the Market in an effort to make Brazilian Jiu-Jitsu available to all of the children practicing martial arts in the United States. He feels that the lessons he's learned from BJJ not only are allowing him to be living the "American Dream" as an Instructor in Sarasota, FL, they are also lessons he wishes to share with the youth of America.

Table of Contents

What it takes to be a good Kid-Jitsu® Instructor

Larry Shealy has been a student of mine for over ten years. He received his purple belt from me and continues to help spread my family's style of Jiu-Jitsu as my Royce Gracie Jiu-Jitsu Network Representative in Jacksonville, Florida. He teaches a very successful adult and youth program there and has a great business background. He is personable and reliable and I am thrilled to have him as a part of my team.

-Royce Gracie
September 2006.

Proverbs 22:6:
"Train up a child in the way he should go,
and when he is old he will not turn from it."

Chapter One
History of Brazilian Jiu-Jitsu

The history is well documented and can be found in many books and is all over the internet. Check out almost any BJJ website and in most cases, the history of Brazilian Jiu-Jitsu can be found there. I will paraphrase the accounts I have read:

Jiu-Jitsu comes to Brazil

In 1914, a Japanese Jiu-Jitsu champion, Count Maeda traveled to Brazil to try to establish a Japanese immigrant community. He was aided by Gastao Gracie, a Brazilian scholar and politician of Scottish descent. As he was grateful for Gastao Gracie's assistance, Maeda taught Gastao Gracie's oldest son, Carlos, the essentials of the art of Japanese Jiu-Jitsu.

After Count Maeda left Brazil to return to Japan, Carlos and his brothers, Oswaldo, Gastao, Jorge and Helio adapted the art and began modifying many of the techniques, throwing out movements that they didn't think worked in street fight scenarios. They had many demonstrations and street fights where their adapted style would soon become the birth of Gracie Jiu-Jitsu.

HELIO GRACIE

Helio Gracie was a small man who as a youngster was quite sickly. He observed his brothers teaching Jiu-Jitsu and over time became a phenomenal teacher himself and a very successful "no holds barred" fighter. Helio is credited for fighting and beating men much bigger and heavier than him. Helio is the father of my Instructor Royce Gracie, as well as Rorion, Relson, Rickson, Rolker, Royler and Robin Gracie.

"When I see the support from the martial arts community in the United States and the way it's growing, I see it as a great thing -- a great future for us, the Americans who learn it and the rest of the world. I wish I had 100 sons so I could [spread the art] faster." -Helio Gracie

ROYCE GRACIE, AND THE U.F.C.

In the late 1980's, Helio Gracie's oldest son, Rorion Gracie, came up with the idea of organizing a no-holds-barred fighting tournament in the United States. This tournament would be in a round robin, single elimination format that would match up style against style: Karate, Sumo, Wrestling, Kung-Fu, Japanese Jiu-Jitsu, Boxing and Gracie Jiu-Jitsu. This was the birth of what is now the U.F.C.: the Ultimate Fighting Championships.

Royce Gracie, in the early U.F.C's changed the way fighters would fight, virtually overnight. He did things in the octagon that people had not seen. They saw a skinny guy, Royce Gracie, beat all comers without throwing any vicious kicks or punches. He beat them on the ground and he did it with Gracie Jiu-Jitsu.

THE U.F.C. TODAY

Fighters in the U.F.C. now are well rounded fighters. They are well versed in wrestling, boxing, Muay Thai and Brazilian Jiu-Jitsu. They are phenomenal athletes and the difference in the U.F.C. today is that it now pits athlete versus athlete, instead of style versus style.

They all seem to be good at it all. And suffice it to say, if they don't know how to fight when on the ground, they will have to learn how in order to be effective in the sport.

Chapter Two
Introduction to Kid-Jitsu®
and The Kid-Jitsu® Values Program

The "Kid-Jitsu® Licensing Program, seminars, workbook and the accompanying DVD set is designed for you, the martial arts business owner and/or Instructor, to be able to effectively implement a children's Brazilian Jiu-Jitsu program into your current curriculum. It does not matter what "style" of martial arts program you instruct, "Kid-Jitsu®": Teaching Children the Art of Brazilian Jiu-Jitsu will allow you to:

- Confidently and thoroughly teach children fundamentally sound principles and techniques of Brazilian Jiu-Jitsu in your school, even if you have never taken or taught Brazilian Jiu-Jitsu before. This book is designed to walk you, the Kid-Jitsu® Instructor, step by step through the entire first year curriculum of "Kid-Jitsu®"

- Retain and/or upgrade more students in your school. You can effectively sell your school as a "Total Self-Defense" School. You can add a ground game to your current curriculum in **as little as two ½ hour classes per week!**

- Take advantage of the popularity of the U.F.C. being on mainstream television. More people are aware of ground fighting and the need for Brazilian Jiu-Jitsu and you too can tap into this market.

- Fill any perceived "void" in some systems that do not offer ground fighting techniques. Offer new streams of revenue for you in sharing in the student licensing fees, upgrades and price increases to your current programs.

- Increase your pro-shop sales with upcoming licensed Kid-Jitsu® Products: T-shirts, Stickers, DVD's, Workbooks, etc.

Chapter Three
Why Kid-Jitsu®?

"Kid-Jitsu®" is the trademarked Brazilian Jiu-Jitsu Program for children at the Jacksonville Brazilian Jiu-Jitsu Academy in Jacksonville, FL. At JaxBJJ we teach Brazilian Jiu-Jitsu, Kid-Jitsu® and Self-Defense techniques in a fun and interactive environment. The techniques are methodically demonstrated and practiced to enhance retention and effectiveness for each child. In addition to this, the **"Kid-Jitsu® Values Program"** is woven throughout each class on a weekly basis.

In addition to the time and reality tested techniques of Brazilian Jiu-Jitsu that is shared with the children; they will also receive the benefits of increased self esteem, self control, self motivation, discipline, better mental focus and many more benefits from the **"Kid-Jitsu® and the Kid-Jitsu® Values Program"**.

Kid-Jitsu® is not a striking art. However it is a great compliment to the striking arts and is a complete Self-Defense System that places emphasis on:

- Proper Position
- Proper Control
- Submissions

Kid-Jitsu® uses control of an attacker instead of striking them. This is similar to the techniques used by Law Enforcement Agencies when arresting criminals. A youngster can use position, control and submission to defend him or herself, without using strikes. By approaching negative situations in this way it allows our children to protect themselves in severe situations, and control the situation without throwing punches and badly hurting their opponent.

Kid-Jitsu® and Karate---should go hand in hand!

"Kid-Jitsu®" and Brazilian Jiu-Jitsu is a "hands on" art. We practice our self-defense techniques full speed, live. In Kid-Jitsu® a child will not need to figure out what to do in a dangerous situation because they practice it in every class in a fun, effective and safe way. Children like action and they like understanding what they are doing…In Kid-Jitsu® they get both and they thrive on it.

Brazilian Jiu-Jitsu is a complete Self-Defense System. A parent cannot be with their children at all times, but they can educate their child on defending themselves. From standing grabs, strikes and abductions to Ground Grappling, Ground Strikes and Submissions, your child will be equipped to defend himself/herself with the fundamental knowledge of Brazilian Jiu-Jitsu that they receive from the "Kid-Jitsu®" Program.

Having a marketing degree and a business background, I have all the respect in the world for the great job that the karate industry does in marketing their programs. In my opinion, most Karate and Martial Arts schools are extremely good at marketing. I have heard some people say that they are marketing machines, and coming from a marketing guy… that is a very good thing! They know and understand what they are doing when it comes to selling their product and providing on going value to their customers.

The implementation of "Kid-Jitsu®" into a karate school or other martial arts curriculum, can cause student retention numbers to go up, and your new student enrollments can reach record highs. A school owner will indeed have the best of both worlds: A good stand-up fighting program and a world renowned ground program for their kids to "complete" their martial arts game.

They will also receive the training and support from the founders of the "Kid-Jitsu®" Program with upcoming "Kid-Jitsu® Certification Seminars, "Kid-Jitsu®" technique DVD's, periodic technical upgrade seminars, and yearly updates to the "Kid-Jitsu®" Curriculum

In this photo are some of our "Kid-Jitsu®" students at JaxBJJ, who visited our Adult Jiu-Jitsu Seminar in June 2006 to meet the Legendary Royce Gracie! The children were thrilled as the ever gracious Royce gave autographs to them all. (Thanks Royce!)

Chapter Four
Training Philosophy
at Jacksonville Brazilian Jiu-Jitsu

Kid-Jitsu®'s Flagship Academy's
Training Philosophy

I believe that it is important for any Martial Arts Academy to not only have a Mission Statement, their short term and long term Financial Goals and Objectives in writing, and a structured business plan ranging out at least 2-3 years; but I also believe that it is equally important for a successful Martial Arts Academy to implement and enforce a philosophy of training. The philosophy is the guideline you can use on how people will train and treat others in your academy. It is a document that can be used proactively to set the guidelines of training and the by-product will be: respectful actions from your students, less activity that can cause injury and or ill will within the school.

There can only be one Chief on the mat and that is the Instructor. Set your expectations of your students high and the culture of your school will be one of respectability and professionalism.
Brazilian Jiu-Jitsu is a "tough" sport and can draw many different and sometimes "unsavory" characters to your Academy. I instituted an "interview" process to my academy and must have "buy-in" to my Philosophy of Training for any Adult to join my school. For the children, I interview the parents to identify the goals and objectives of what their expectations are and what I will be able to provide in our program. I have turned people away because they just did not "fit" the culture of the school we have developed. One bad apple may not ruin

the entire bunch, but in a martial arts academy they can do much more damage than their monthly payment is worth.

Although this philosophy doesn't necessarily apply to the "Kid-Jitsu®" program, I feel it is important to note that we do have a family oriented business with women, children and professionals participating in our Brazilian Jiu-Jitsu Program. The tone and professionalism of your school and your "Kid-Jitsu®" program can be established with the implementation of this type philosophy. The parents read it and understand where I am coming from as a school owner and as their children's instructor.

Having had the potential to read and "buy-in" to this thought-process, the discipline of an out of control student is quite easy. It's as simple as a conversation that you have with that student that says: "These are the expectations and you are not following them. What can you do to change your actions?" This puts the ball in their court and allows you the opportunity to "fix" the situation, and move forward.

The key to discipline in the adults and the children's classes are in being consistent and predictable, which we will discuss more in Chapter 9.

Below is a copy of the Training Philosophy that I have implemented in my school. I keep a stack of copies of them in our reception area. I refer to it every day in discussions with prospective students.

Jacksonville Brazilian Jiu-Jitsu, Inc. Training Philosophy

Welcome to Team JaxBjj, a Royce Gracie Jiu-Jitsu Training Academy. Brazilian Jiu-Jitsu was perfected by Helio Gracie due to his slight frame and his inability to perform the moves that required a great deal of strength and explosive power in traditional Japanese Jiu-Jitsu. His use of leverage and technique allowed him to compete with and conquer opponents in Vale Tudo fights that were much larger, faster and stronger than him. Helio's son and my Instructor, Royce, has further proved the simple effectiveness of Brazilian Jiu-Jitsu in his many No-Hold's Barred victories in The Ultimate Fighting Championships as well his Pride Championship Fights in Japan.

We believe that training Brazilian Jiu-Jitsu should be practiced in the same way that the Gracie's have trained: with consistent and intelligent practice, with instruction that comes directly from the Gracie source, with impeccable technique, with constant repetition and with excellent use of leverage and timing versus strength and explosiveness.

We believe in training hard and training smart. Our philosophy is to "train for 30 years, not 30 minutes." Thus, safety and knowing when to "tap" is paramount. Senseless injuries have never made anyone a better Jiu-Jitsu Player!

We believe that you should check your ego at the door when training Brazilian Jiu-Jitsu. It's not if you win, or if you submit the most people in a given training session; it's if you have learned anything and improved on your own abilities in every training session. Training is for learning and improving your game while helping your training partners get better as well. Fighting is for competition. Please know the difference and be a good training partner!

We believe that in training Gracie Brazilian Jiu-Jitsu, you will get out of it in direct proportion to what you put in to it. Commit to training and put the hours in on the mat and you will indeed improve and you will carry yourself accordingly.

We believe that Gracie Brazilian Jiu-Jitsu is the most complete and effective martial art available. We believe you have come to the right place to learn and train and we believe that you, too, can be a CHAMPION, in all aspects of your life.

Good luck and Good Training!

- Larry Shealy, M.B.A.
Owner and Head Instructor
Jacksonville Brazilian Jiu-Jitsu, Inc.
a Royce Gracie Jiu-Jitsu Academy
www.jaxbjj.com

Thoughts on having a training philosophy

I believe that a solid training philosophy is a pre-requisite to a successful Brazilian Jiu-Jitsu Program. I know, without a doubt, that this simple document alone and the promotion of the contents has made my school enrollment numbers increase by leaps and bounds. Why? Because people know that they can trust me and my current students to have their well being and safety in mind, and they also have a guideline for training that they can abide by.

You probably recall your first visit to a martial arts academy. It was probably intimidating to you. It sure was for me. My goal at my school is to be a highly effective and technical school. I also make a consistent effort in dealing with difficult students and their parents <u>before</u> any problems begin to affect the school.

I have had to ask a few people to train somewhere else. The circumstances were that their goals and objectives did not match with what I was trying to accomplish at the Academy. I did not have any hard feelings towards them. I was just making a sound business decision.

So far, so good on this policy and I highly recommend this approach with a BJJ curriculum in your school.

Chapter Five
Putting the Kid in Brazilian Jiu-Jitsu

Why "Kid-Jitsu®"?

"Kid-Jitsu®" is the perfect compliment to many of the Karate Curriculum's that are in place today throughout the world. The beautiful thing about "Kid-Jitsu®" is that the techniques work for children of all sizes, shapes, temperaments and athletic ability. One does not have to be big, strong, fast or athletically gifted to become quite proficient in Brazilian Jiu-Jitsu, and more specifically "Kid-Jitsu®"

Having grown up in a "tough" neighborhood and having been "picked on" by a merciless older brother who was 5 years older than me, I feel it is important to equip all children to be able to protect themselves. I wish I had known Brazilian Jiu-Jitsu in my early childhood years! Not to have hurt people or to have beaten them up, but to have been able to neutralize abusive situations with an older brother and the bullies in my neighborhood!

As parents, children are a gift from God to us all. As a school owner, the children are gifts to our businesses. I believe they are much, much more than a dollar sign and so are their parents. It is our responsibility as martial arts instructors to prepare these children to **defend themselves** in a hostile situation. I believe that making money is a by-product of the superior services that we sell. We aren't selling belts, we are selling knowledge, we are selling safety and we are selling piece of mind to the parents. The belts are the by-product of all the work that we have done with the children and all the work that the children have done toward their individual goals.

I can lay my head down at night and I know in my heart that I am preparing my Kid-Jitsu® students for the worst case self-defense scenarios with the techniques of Brazilian Jiu-Jitsu. I am also preparing them to be the "best that they can be" with the Kid-Jitsu® Values Program.

I ask myself a few questions, day in and day out:

- Am I teaching my Kid-Jitsu® students how to defend themselves?
- Am I helping them to be better people?
- Am I leading them by example?

Kid-Jitsu® can be an "add-on" to the many fine martial arts programs that are simply   looking to add Brazilian Jiu-Jitsu program to their current system.

Please consider my input on this as a means of adding to what is being done in your program. I believe you can use Brazilian Jiu-Jitsu as a spring board to a more well- rounded program that indeed covers all bases for our kids.

Structuring your Kid-Jitsu® Program

We all need structure in our lives or we find chaos everywhere. Kid's need structure more than we care to admit.

Put a group of children together, without structure, and the action increases, the sounds reach ear piercingly high decibels and someone invariably will get hurt and it does not take long to watch and see this sequence of events occur.

Structure: Who is the boss?

This one is easy. I am the boss in my school and everyone knows this. It is not an obnoxious feeling of superiority that I display. It is just a well engineered and implemented system of establishing a hierarchy in the school. It is based on mutual respect, compassion and love. It is based on structure, discipline, consistency and predictability.

After only a class or two, there is no doubt in the children's or their parent's mind that Mr. Larry is the boss.

On a daily basis, as soon as my kids begin arriving for class, they will begin seeing that the structure of that day's program will be the same as previous classes. They will also immediately see that my actions toward them, and my expectations of them being well behaved, will be exactly the same as in previous classes.

I set my expectations very high for my kids. It is totally my responsibility to set the tone for that day's class, and the expectations that I have for them.

No matter where I set my expectations for my students, they will always rise to that level. If I set them low, they will perform at a low level. If I set the expectations high, they will perform at a high level. Since my goal is having a superior program, with superior students I must always set my expectations very high for myself, my assistants and my students.

What are my expectations?

My expectations of the children are simple. I expect the following from each child in the class:

- Respect for me and the other students
- Good manners
- Self-Control
- Self-Discipline
- A kind and gentle spirit
- A willingness to learn

The children in my program are abundantly clear on the fact that I am the boss. They know my expectations for them and they know that if they don't follow the rules and the expectations that I set for them, there will be consequences. Hindu squats and push-ups help keep this point clear in their minds in just about every class!

Discipline in your school

Now that I have set the expectations that I have for the children's behavior, and I have set the rules of the road for the class, what do I do now?

There must be consequences for inappropriate behavior. I'm not going to tell you how to run your discipline within your curriculum, but I will share a few parameters that you will most likely want to implement, if they are not already set in your program.

Being Consistent and Predictable with discipline

In my first sales management job in my previous career, I received some advice from my Regional Manager that was some of the best "people" advice that I have ever received. He told be that when managing people we need to be always be: **"consistent and predictable"** in all of our dealings with them. Over time, I found this to be some of the most valuable information I could have received as a new sales manager. It has also proven to be valuable information in dealing with my own children, and in my "Kid-Jitsu®" Program. (Thank you Evans Wisner for this valuable truth—I miss you man! You left this earth way too early!!!)

You see, once we set the rules and have made the rules known to our students we must be:

- **Consistent** in enforcing the rules.
- And, **predictable** in how we will enforce the rules.

This takes the guesswork out of the equation for us and our students. In any given situation we know how we are going to handle that situation. It also gives the children the upfront knowledge of what to expect from us as their teachers in any given situation.

Be consistent and predictable with your encouragement and praise

This is the area where most discipline programs fall flat on their face. Discipline without the backdrop of love, encouragement and praise will fail every time.

Discipline with only consequences of poor behavior is a recipe for disaster. If you pour all the water out of a bucket, the inside of the bucket will "dry out". If you don't pour the "water of encouragement" into a child you will "dry out" or break their spirit.

When we set our expectations of the children in our schools we don't only tell the children what not to do and what is bad; we must also show and tell them what behaviors are good and what good behaviors are expected of them. The Kid-Jitsu values program engrains "good behaviors" into them over time.

In this way of thinking it is our obligation to "catch them doing something good." I've found that by providing encouragement and praise of specific behaviors, even the worst behaved children can deliver positive results over time.

Putting it together

Draw two lines on a sheet of paper parallel to each other from the top of the page to the bottom of the page. You could envision the area between these two lines as being a highway. On the outside of the right line write "good" and on the outside of the left line write "bad". These two lines represent good behavior and bad behavior and it can simply be your "roadmap" for your discipline program.

When you catch a person on the left side of the road it represents bad behavior you must immediately address the behavior with the student.

When you catch a person on the right side of the road it represents them doing something good and you must immediately praise and encourage them for their good behavior.

This road map takes the guesswork out of your discipline in your school. If you are simply "consistent and predictable" in administering the discipline in your school, you will see amazing results.

The Fantastic Five F's in your successful "Kid-Jitsu®" Program

- Fun
- Friendly
- Family
- Fundamentals
- Full of Integrity

Fun in Kid-Jitsu®

Once I have laid down the "laws" of our Kid-Jitsu® program, the hard part is over. I have the discipline program in place. Now is the time for the **FUN**! My personal style is to use a lot of humor and connect with my children with the use of humor. I use nicknames, I get on their level and get to know their interests and simply talk to them. Kids just love to have fun and making it fun for them can make it fun for you. Have fun, laugh, make them laugh. A little laugher goes a very long way in making children enjoy their Kid-Jitsu® Classes.

Friendliness in Kid-Jitsu®

The golden rule is a good way to do things in any situation where more than one person is involved. As humans, we can find incredible ways NOT to get along. This is not an option in Kid-Jitsu®. The expectation is set that everyone is friendly to one another. Even when people are just arriving to class, they come to the center of the mat all facing each other. There are no cliques, no groups and no children being ostracized. The children, after being shown that small groups are not allowed, embrace it and go with the flow.

To paraphrase the Golden Rule that we follow: "Do unto others, the way that you would have them do unto you."

Simply put: we treat people in Kid-Jitsu® the way that we want to be treated!!!! There are no other options!

Family in Kid-Jitsu®

I treat my students like one big family. We've established no cliques and no secret groups. I am the father in the family and my assistants are the big brothers and the big sisters. We all know the rules, we know the guidelines, we know when we can have fun and we know when it's time to work.

Family: I treat the kids like family. Before class I sit on the mat with them and talk and try to "get into their world, on their level." It is amazing what these children will share with you when you take time with them.

Fundamentals in Kid-Jitsu®

The techniques in the Kid-Jitsu® Program are a set of fundamentals that when practiced over time will allow the children to take care of them selves. We practice the fundamentals with tremendous amounts of repetition over a long period of time. We do not get hung up with learning hundreds of techniques with 26% proficiency. We practice 26 fundamental techniques and acquire 100% proficiency.

Full of Integrity in Kid-Jitsu®

Our children simply cannot help but develop their fundamental jiu-jitsu skills in the Kid-Jitsu® Program; as they practice the techniques over and over in a repetitive manner over a long period of time.

The same holds true with developing Integrity in the Kid-Jitsu® Program. We sit down and discuss 1 of 26 values on a weekly basis. We discuss the value, get a feel for what the value is, how it is applied and we follow-up with the Kid-Jitsu® Value of the week at every class. I ask the kids questions like:

- What is (for example) Honesty?
- Can you give an example of a situation where you demonstrated honesty in the past few days?
- How did that make you feel?
- Have you ever not been honest?
- What was it that you were not honest about?
- How did that make you feel?

I always give the children a homework assignment for the week. The assignment is to come back to class the next time with an example from the Value of the Week, and how it was used. They are also encouraged to share their example with the group.

Chapter Six
Dealing with the Parents

What do parents want for their children when they place them in a Martial Arts Program?

I believe that parents are looking for a complete development system for their children. I believe they are looking for their children to be involved with other children, learn social skills, learn some of life's "values", and have some fun, in addition to learning a martial art.

"Kid-Jitsu®" provides many of the qualities in our program that the parents are wanting for their children.

I am going to use the acronym **K.I.D.-J.I.T.S.U.** to discuss some of the qualities that I believe parents are looking for in a martial arts program:

Kindness: the Golden Rule
Integrity: building integrity into their children.
Determination and Discipline: a "can-do" attitude and the desire for them to complete the various activities that they have begun.
Justice: their children will be treated in a fair and just manner.
Inspiration: being inspired to accomplish your goals.
Teamwork: working well with others.
Self-Defense: being able to handle one's self in a crisis situation.
Understanding: understanding structure, discipline and a chain of command.

In Kid-Jitsu® we are dedicated to assisting in developing the well being and character and integrity of every student that attends our school.

The proof is in the pudding! Develop a testimonial base.

It is easy to toot your own horn, but to develop trust in your program you must develop a testimonial base for other parents to read. Below you can read through some of the unsolicited testimonials that I have received from the parents of some of my "Kid-Jitsu®" students. I also put these on my website for potential students to read. Nobody can sell your program as well as satisfied customers! Here are a few that I pulled from my website:

Testimonials

Larry, Thanks so much for your continued professionalism; your discipline is impeccable with the children. They truly have a coach and mentor, that has a magnificent outlook on life and is installing the kind of morals and self confidence a parent needs in their children. Because of you J.'s hard work paid off and because of you all our children get to experience a bit of greatness. Thanks so much!

The L. Family

....

Larry, I just wanted to pass on a thank you, K. is having a great time, it's all she talks about now. What you are doing with these children will be a building block for the rest of their lives...THANK YOU SO MUCH!!!!!

L. H. Jacksonville Florida

....

I have twin boys (9 years old) who are currently going to "Kid-Jitsu". They thoroughly enjoy it and can't wait to go to every class that Larry offers. One of my sons is very shy and has been diagnosed with ADHD for 5 years. My wife and I were at our wits end with how to keep him focused on school and his behavior. We had tried everything from medications, to a lot of suggestions form his pediatrician, to no avail. Since attending Larry's Kid-Jitsu program he has excelled at school and his behavior has been impecable. His self-confidence is soaring daily. Both of the boys love the sport and I am as proud as any father can be of them. Larry teaches the kids respect for others, self respect and alot of life lessons that they can use forever. Most importantly the kids have FUN. Larry and Kid-Jitsu has been a blessing to our family. Thank you Larry and Gail.

Jim G.—Jacksonville, Florida

The passion, pride and camaraderie my children have experienced with Larry Shealy's Royce Gracie Jiu-Jitsu Academy have been inspiring. These traits coupled with the increased confidence and discipline makes this experience a true gem.

C. T., Jacksonville, Florida

My daughter has benefited in many ways from the Kid-Jitsu program; physically, mentally and emotionally. Learning the jiu-jitsu moves has boosted her confidence to continue to learn more. And learning to respect each other and looking into their partners eyes is such a neat thing to see these little ones doing. Most of all they have so much fun! They all love Mr. Larry!

D. M. Jacksonville, FL

I can't say enough about the positive experience my two boys, ages 6 & 7, have had in working with Larry Shealy and the entire staff at Kid-Jitsu! It's apparent that Larry and his team have a dedication and commitment to developing young people in positive ways. The boys absolutely love Kid-Jitsu, and look forward to every "training session!" There's not a single young person I know who wouldn't benefit from learning basic self defense *techniques in this sort of a structured, disciplined environment. I highly recommend Larry Shealy and Kid-Jitsu!"*

G. Z.—Jacksonville, Florida

....

I have been training at JaxBJJ for over a year now. I specifically like the great workout I receive and the competitive nature of Brazilian Jiu-Jitsu, as I am a very competitive person. In the past few months I have been bringing my 12 year old son T. W. with me to training.and he love's it. His self-esteem has soared since he began training, he's "toughening up" mentally and physically and he's learning the solid fundamentals of Gracie Jiu-Jitsu. We are planning to be the first father-son team at JaxBJJ to compete together at upcoming Tournament/Grappling Competitions.

J.W.—Jacksonville, Florida

....

RESPECT: The cornerstone of good human relations

Aretha Franklin wrote about R-E-S-P-E-C-T., in a song titled "Respect" that was released in 1967. I'm going to write a little about respect and how it is a "must have" in any program that has people working together.

I truly believe that respect is indeed the cornerstone to good human relations. It allows people of different backgrounds, social classes, and cultures to have a common thread to allow them to get along with one another.

Respect is not an option in my school. All of my students are required to show proper respect to all adults, authority figures, fellow students and themselves. This is not an option. I show respect for ALL of the people who come into my school: parents, children, students, visitors. I am a firm believer in "practicing" what you preach and I certainly preach respect on a daily and weekly basis.

"Kid-Jitsu®" Student Creed

I intend to develop myself in a positive manner and avoid anything that will reduce my physical health and mental growth.

I intend to develop my self-discipline to bring out the best in myself and others.

I intend to use what I learn in class constructively and defensively to help myself and others and to never be abusive or offensive.

(Obtained from EFC, Educational Funding Company)

All of my students must memorize and recite the creed before the class within the first month of their joining my Academy. We also recite it together at the end of each class, and when we bow out, we bow out with the word "RESPECT!

Chapter Seven
The Mat Doesn't Lie

Bear with me on this as the belt progression in Brazilian Jiu-Jitsu, as far as I have seen is not what one would call an exact science. I will explain the Adult Belts first, and that should put some things in perspective as then I will cover the belts in the "Kid-Jitsu®" belt progression.

The Adult Belt Progression in Brazilian Jiu-Jitsu

In Brazilian Jiu-Jitsu you are promoted by being able to compete with and or beat people at your level. If, as an adult, you are a blue belt and you train with blue belts and beat them, eventually (nobody knows when!) you will be promoted and over time you will attain the next belt level. Suffice it to say that if your desire is in receiving belts quickly, then BJJ is probably not the martial art for you. Attaining a higher belt level does not necessarily mean more moves or techniques. You will learn most of the techniques in a relatively short period of time. The advancement in Brazilian Jiu-Jitsu is in direct relation to your execution of the techniques and the time you have accumulated on the mat....... mat time.

My instructor, Royce Gracie has a couple of phrases that he has coined about the belting process, two of which I'll share with you. In discussing the belt system with me several years ago he said to look at the belts in this way:

"White belt, blue belt...forget about it!"

What do you think Royce Gracie meant by this statement? At the time I really didn't understand what he meant. He has a way of making simple sounding statements, that at the time do not make sense, but over time they not only make sense, they are quite profound.

Royce meant that you should work hard and often and work on the techniques that he teaches. I had earned the blue belt already and this was his way of saying, Larry, work hard and perfect the techniques I show you and with precision in utilizing the techniques, the belts will come over time.

In Brazilian Jiu-Jitsu, the mat does not lie!

Brazilian Jiu-Jitsu has a no-nonsense approach to belts. When you reach a level of proficiency in the techniques and their applications in "real" sparring and situations, you will receive a new belt. When you receive a particular belt, you must be able to compete on the mat with others who are the same belt level. **The mat does not lie!**

Another quote attributed to Royce Gracie puts this thought process totally into perspective:

The belt only covers 2" of you're a!!, the rest you've got to back up on your own!"

That pretty much sums it up. You earn your belt and must be able to back it up on the mat.

Also in Brazilian Jiu-Jitsu it really isn't about the belt at all. It is about learning each day you come to class. Enjoy the successes that you have on the mat and don't beat yourself up over your defeats. It's about being technical and smooth and not going ballistic and becoming exhausted in the first few minutes of training. It's a very humbling sport and it's also a very rewarding sport.

It is important as the Instructor of your "Kid-Jitsu®" Program that you understand this and share it with your students.

It's not about the belt…it's about knowledge and performance.

It's not about athleticism…it's about technique.
It's not about strength…it's about leverage.
It's not about who submits who …it's about learning something every class.

Once again, in Brazilian Jiu-Jitsu, the mat does not lie!

The GOOD NEWS: The "Kid-Jitsu®" Belt System

Now that I've got that off of my chest, I have good news!!! The Kid-Jitsu®" System has several belts for the children to work through. Please review the picture of the entire Brazilian Jiu-Jitsu Belt System.

Belt Progression in Brazilian Jiu-Jitsu

Listed below is the belt progression within the Gracie Jiu-Jitsu system. As Royce Gracie is my instructor, this is the belt progression that I use in my school.

As a Licensed "Kid-Jitsu®" School, you also will use the "Kid-Jitsu®" belt progression that is listed on the following page:

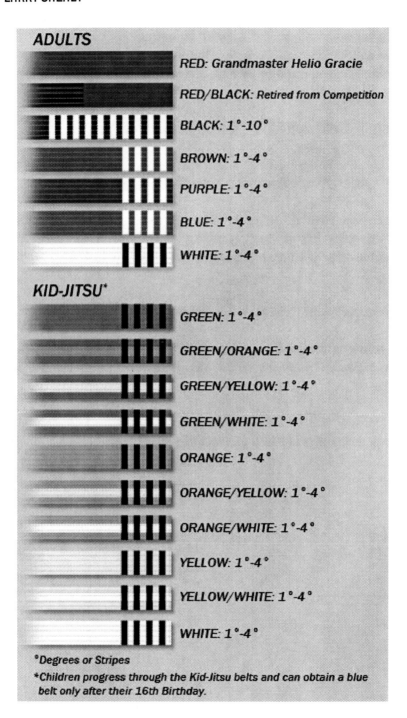

ADULTS

RED: *Grandmaster Helio Gracie*

RED/BLACK: Retired from Competition

BLACK: 1°-10°

BROWN: 1°-4°

PURPLE: 1°-4°

BLUE: 1°-4°

WHITE: 1°-4°

KID-JITSU*

GREEN: 1°-4°

GREEN/ORANGE: 1°-4°

GREEN/YELLOW: 1°-4°

GREEN/WHITE: 1°-4°

ORANGE: 1°-4°

ORANGE/YELLOW: 1°-4°

ORANGE/WHITE: 1°-4°

YELLOW: 1°-4°

YELLOW/WHITE: 1°-4°

WHITE: 1°-4°

°Degrees or Stripes

*Children progress through the Kid-Jitsu belts and can obtain a blue belt only after their 16th Birthday.

"Kid-Jitsu®" Belt Progression

The "Kid-Jitsu®" Belt System is a very motivating belt system for the children to measure their successes and their progress in the art of Brazilian Jiu-Jitsu.

We realize that children thrive on goal setting and goal achieving and the feelings of accomplishment as each goal is reached.

We will fully discuss children's promotions "Kid-Jitsu®" in detail when we work together on your certification. However, in a nutshell, the children will receive a stripe for every six classes attended, provided that he/she masters the material provided over this timeframe. Each belt has 4 degrees or stripes and a new belt will be awarded with a minimum of 24 classes attended, and mastering of the material covered during that time. This progression usually takes about 3-4 months.

Also please note, in the "Kid-Jitsu®" Program, the highest belt a child can achieve is the Green Belt with 4 stripes. If a child is a Green Belt with 4 stripes, they can then be considered for a blue belt upon their 16th birthday, and only from a qualified Brazilian Jiu-Jitsu Instructor. The road to Green Belt should be about a 3-4 year process and is a VERY significant achievement in our system.

Example: In the early years of my current school I only had adult classes. A father, begged for me to let his son train with us, despite him being only ten years old. He was very young and very small. I let him train with us as kind of our "mascot." After a few years he got pretty good in Brazilian Jiu-Jitsu. By the time he was 14 years of age he weighed close to 130 pounds and he had attained the green belt level. He dominated the competition circuit in his age group and submitted his opponents, usually in short order. At 13 years old he was hitting "flying arm bars" and "flying triangles" during competition. To say he was very good at BJJ would be a huge understatement.

It got to a point where he could tap about 60% of my ADULT students!!! He worked hard and he learned the fundamentals using no muscle. (he had no muscle to use!) Add that to the fact that he was a child among men, he simply had to master the techniques. Needless to say when he turns 16, he will get his Blue Belt.

I cannot stress how big of an event it is for a child to reach the green belt level. Their proficiency in Brazilian Jiu-Jitsu at this point is STRONG! To coin a phrase, I'd say that the "***Green Belt is the Children's Black Belt in Brazilian Jiu-Jitsu.***"

Chapter Eight
From Arm Bars to UPA:
The Kid-Jitsu® Curriculum

Note: <u>The techniques portion of this book will specifically bullet point each of the techniques of the "Kid-Jitsu®" curriculum. It is meant to work in conjunction with and as an outline for the "Kid-Jitsu®" DVD's.</u>

<u>Please refer to your DVD's and follow along with the outline as you watch the DVD's. The visual of the DVD's and the bullet points, which you can and should add to in your own words, will help you retain and be able to effectively perform and teach each of the fundamental techniques to your "Kid-Jitsu®" Students.</u>

"Kid-Jitsu®" Fundamentals

Brazilian Jiu-Jitsu can be a frustrating sport to learn. It can be frustrating because the benefits of the sport: no need to be strong, fast or athletically gifted, also can be the double edged sword of the sport. Those who are accustomed to muscling their way through various sports will soon grow frustrated in Brazilian Jiu-Jitsu. That is, until they give up on the muscling through the techniques long enough to learn the proper fundamentals of Brazilian Jiu-Jitsu.

Understanding base and leverage:

Grand Master Helio Gracie is a genius the way he modified Japanese Jiu-Jitsu to be effective for his small and less than intimidating body frame. He figured out that for him to survive against larger and stronger opponents in the fight world, he had to use every God-given advantage that, though unseen, he possessed.

What Helio figured out, was that by proper use of his body weight, his balance and application of his body weight and the leverage he could generate with his body weight, he could not only hang in there with larger and stronger opponents, he could beat them in vale tudo, no holds barred fighting.

What is base and what is leverage?

In my "Kid-Jitsu®" classes you will attend and in the DVD's you will hear me talk a lot about base, and posture and leverage. These are terms that are the life's blood of Brazilian Jiu-Jitsu.

I will put these terms in my own "Kid-Jitsu®" terms that will not be found in Webster's dictionary!

- **Base** is the proper balance and proper use of your body weight.

- **Posture** means to utilize the balance and weight of your body not to be thrown off balance.

- **Leverage** in this instance will be the use of your body control and angles without using your physical strength, to be able to move your opponent to a position you wish to put him in. Leverage is not power!

As coaches it is up to us to not only teach the appropriate techniques, but to also monitor each students progress and assist them in perfecting their grappling game. Make sure that they are paired with other students of equal size and ability.

As you begin teaching "Kid-Jitsu®" you must constantly stress the importance of use of base and leverage and technique and also stress that strength should not be applied in any of these techniques.

Once the techniques are committed to muscle memory then strength may be applied as a bonus. The beautiful thing about Brazilian Jiu-Jitsu and "Kid-Jitsu®" is that size and strength really do not matter. The smaller man, woman or child with superior technique can and does beat the larger, less technical opponent; and that my friend is a beautiful thing!

The Fundamentals of "Kid-Jitsu®"

The 26 Fundamental Techniques of "Kid-Jitsu®"—Level I
Please note: For demonstration purposes I have chronicled the 26 moves as a right handed person. If you are left handed and wish to use your "strong" side, anytime I say right hand, just replace it with the left hand and vice versa.

8.1. Defend Being Grabbed: One Handed

Objective: resist and escape

Immediate Danger: being taken to another site

When grabbed:
- Drop in base. Your feet and legs will be perpendicular to the feet, and legs of your attacker.
- Raise the arm that is grabbed and lean forward and at the same time pointing your elbow up and toward your attacker.
- You will gently rotate the thin part of your wrist between the attackers thumb and forefinger, breaking the grip.
- Run away from the attacker
- Practice this technique slow, and with precision.
- Optional technique 1: open hand to the ear
- Optional technique 2: the "circle" technique

Common mistakes:
1. Not dropping correctly in base
2. Pulling the arm away versus using a can opener effect
3. Not twisting the skinny part of the arm past the thumb and forefinger of the attacker.

8.2. Defend Being Grabbed - with Two Hands

Objective: resist and escape

Immediate Danger: being taken to another site

Technique:
Similar to move #1, but this time the attacker grabs your arm with both hands like he is gripping a baseball bat:
- Immediately drop in base.
- Ball a fist with the arm that is grabbed
- Maintain base and reach over your fist and grab your fist.
- Moving your base from your front foot to your back foot pulling both of your hands across your body, escaping from the grasp of your attacker.
- Run away from the attacker.

Optional technique: Open hand to the ear if the opponent is still within range as you escape his grasp.

Common Mistakes:
1. Not dropping in base properly.
2. Not firming up the grabbed wrist with a balled fist. (could break wrist)
3. Forgetting to reach over and grab with the second hand.

8.3. Defend Against the Front Choke

Objective: protect trachea and escape

Immediate Danger: thumbs on trachea

Technique:
- Immediately tuck your chin into your chest pinning your chin against his thumbs.
- As you begin stepping back in base lower your head straight down toward your feet and making a big "U" with your head as you pass your head underneath his arm.
- By forcing your head down you will open his thumbs and by making a "U" with your head you will pass under and around his arms to make your escape.
- By stepping back in base you are creating leverage, distance from your attacker and are setting up for the open hand to the ear.
- Deliver the open hand to your attacker's ear, temporarily stunning him.
- Run away from your attacker.

Common mistakes:
1. Not making a deep enough 'U' with the head
2. Backing straight back versus backing into base.
3. Trying to pull away

8.4 Take Downs: Single Leg.

Objective: take your opponent to the ground.

Immediate Danger: being kneed in the face.

Technique: **"touch—step—grab—lift—walk"** which I have the children repeat as they begin doing takedowns.

Close the gap and avoid knees by:
- Touch—be close enough to touch your opponent.
- Step-toward your opponent
- Grab-grab his knee with both hands and "hug it".
- Lift-Lift his leg up as tight as you can.
- Walk—walk him off and dump him to the ground.
- Trip with other foot if necessary
- Follow your opponent to the ground
- Maintain a dominant position

Though this is perhaps overly simplistic, it gives the kids a planned strategy and a means for getting their opponent onto the ground.

Common mistakes:
1. Not moving quickly enough to the leg.
2. Not lifting and driving forward at the same time.
3. Walking the opponent around in a circle.

8.5 Osoto Gari

Objective: take your opponent to the ground.

Immediate Danger: being taken to the ground, losing your balance.

Technique:
- Control your opponents left side lapel up near his neck with thumb in
- Control the cloth behind his right elbow.
- As you step slightly to the right, pull with your left hand that has his elbow and push with your right hand into his face neck area as if you are turning a big steering wheel. (See DVD)
- As you do this he will become a little off balance, step thru with your right leg and place it behind his right leg.
- Continue to "turn the big wheel", twisting him over and past your right leg and onto the ground.

Common mistakes:
- The wrong grips
- Not "turning the big wheel"
- Improper Footwork

8.6 UPA
(Pronounced: ooh-puh)

Objective: reverse the position, getting your opponent off of you.

Immediate danger: punches to the face and head while you are mounted.

UPA is used when someone is mounted on top of you as you lay flat on your back. Picture the bully on the playground pinning another child and holding his hands to the ground. This is a very precarious situation that needs to be reversed immediately to neutralize the attack.

Technique: (modified for Kids):
- Relax with your elbows pinned to the ground and against your ribs.
- Grab one of his sleeves with both of your hands and hold on very tight.
- Put your foot next to his foot on the same side as the arm you grabbed: if you are controlling his right arm by the sleeve, put your left foot next to his right foot.
- Put your feet up near your butt and thrust your hips up toward the ceiling, as his weight moves over you, push your hips INTO the side that his arm and leg are trapped.
- This will put you into the guard position. If he is not trained, step over his legs and mount him
- If he wraps his legs, begin to immediately pass his guard.

Options:
1. If he is choking you—control his arm and hook his foot and upa.
2. If his arms are on the ground, reach up and around one arm, hook the same side foot and upa.

Common mistakes:
1. Not controlling arm and/or leg on the same side of his body
2. Trying to roll the wrong way
3. Pushing to the side instead of over your head and then to the side.
4. Pushing into his chest, giving him the arm bar.

8.7 Elbow Escape

Objective: reverse the position back to guard, or to your opponent's back.

Immediate danger: punches to your face and head.

Technique:
Using the leverage in your hips, hip out to one side:
- As you pin your elbow on the inside of one of his knees.
- As space is created pull your knee in toward the elbow you used to base off of his knee
- This has created some space
- Plant the same foot and hip out to the other side, again pulling your knee toward you chest. This will put him back into your guard.

Common mistakes:
1. Trying to use upper body strength with your arms instead of using the hips as leverage to separate his knees and create space.
2. Trying to hip out without being prepared to draw a knee up and through to catch him in half guard.
3. Getting trapped on the ground after catching half guard.

8.8 Scissor Sweep

Objective: to reverse your position from guard to mount.

Immediate danger: opponent passing your guard.

Technique:
- Control his right collar with your right hand
- Control his right sleeve with your left hand
- Drag your right knee across his belly hooking your right foot on his hip.
- Move his weight forward and over you and scissor your legs to reverse him
- You will follow him to the mounted position.

Common mistakes:
1. Incorrect grips and hand positions
2. Staying flat on your back.
3. Working against your own body instead of using his body's momentum and your leverage.

8.9 Guard Pass: Gracie Pass

Objective: to gain a superior position

Immediate danger: triangle or arm bar

Technique:
- While you are in your opponents guard, control your opponent's hips and confirm them to the ground.
- While keeping your posture, post up your left leg and lean back into his ankles putting pressure on his ankles.
- As he opens his legs, post your left hand to the ground (putting your hand between his leg and your body, down to the ground)
- Walk your fingers on the mat up toward his head and "shrug" his leg up to your shoulder.
- Keep your posture, keeping your head and neck well above his knee. (to prevent the triangle)
- Reach your left arm across his body, placing the thumb of your left hand into his far collar.
- While putting pressure on his neck for the choke, drive your body weight in a linear fashion, stacking his body weight up onto his neck.
- As he is totally stacked, lean into his legs and let them fall across your face.
- You will end up in the side mount.

Common mistakes:
1. Leaving arms extended into his mid-line and above.
2. Not controlling his hips.
3. Not controlling his second arm at the bicep if he places his first hand in your collar   for a front choke.
4. Stacking across his body instead of linear to his body.
5. Thumb not in the collar and not forcing the choke as you pass the guard.

8.10 Guard Pass: Knee Across

Objective: to gain a superior control position

Immediate danger: being swept

Technique:
- Control your opponents hips and confirm them to the ground
- Place one hand (or both hands for smaller children) on your opponent's right knee and push down with all your body weight.
- As his knee goes down place your right knee across his right thigh, trapping it on the ground between your right knee and right ankle.
- Keep your body weight on him using your right side and under hook his left arm with your right arm, pulling yourself around to side mount.

Common mistakes:
1. Not controlling his hips.
2. Not controlling his bicep if he has one hand in for the choke.
3. Not keeping your body weight on him.
4. Not keeping his leg trapped between you knee and ankle.

8.11 Side Control

Objective: control and set up mount or submission

Immediate danger: opponent going back to guard or to his knees to escape.

Technique:
As you pass the guard and establish your base:
- Place your left hand across their body and put your left arm flat on the ground with your elbow against your opponent's ear.
- Place your right arm against their hip on the near side posted on the mat.

Common mistakes:
1. Not placing your bottom hand on the near side next to his hip on the mat, allowing him to pull you back to guard.
2. Allowing too much space and allowing opponent to get up to his knees.

8.12 Choke from Side Control

Objective: to finish the fight by submission

Immediate danger: opponent can turn into you and reach your leg for reversal.

Technique:
As you maintain base in side control:
- Lift your left hand and place your thumb in this far collar.
- Ball your fist and control a good grip on his collar.
- Bring the blade of the forearm across his neck as if you were using it as a paper cutter.
- Continue this until he taps.
- If he does not tap, maintain the pressure on his neck and point your elbow up toward the top of his head until he taps.

Common mistakes:
1. Not placing your choking hand in deep enough.
2. Not placing the blade of the arm across the neck

8.13 Mount: Drag Knee

Objective: to gain a superior position.

Immediate danger: being put into half-guard.

Technique:
As you "bug his neck" with the choke from side control:
- Place your right hand across his body near his hip to maintain your balance.
- Place your right knee on his belly just above his hip line and drive your knee to the other side of his body.
- You are now mounted.
- Let go of the choke and place your hands on the mat above his head to maintain your base and to maintain the mount.

Common mistakes
1. Forgetting to bug his neck.
2. Jumping instead of dragging the knee.
3. Not getting the hands to the mat in time to base before being reversed.

8.14 Mount: Leg Over

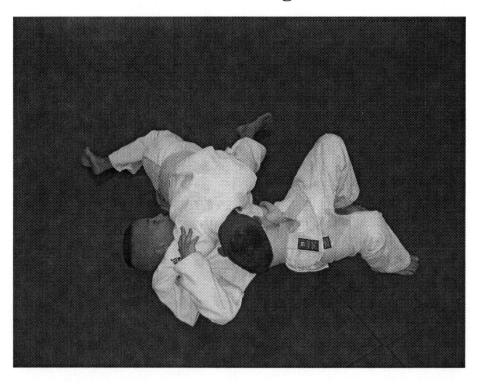

Objective: to gain a superior position, mount

Immediate danger: being reversed, half guard

Technique:
As you continue to "bug his neck" from side control:
- Maintaining your weight on his chest, splay your legs and lay on your right side.
- Your left leg is now parallel to his right leg
- And your right leg is perpendicular to his body
- Throw your right leg over his body as quickly as you can to maintain a mounted position
- Establish your base.

Common mistakes:
1. Not getting the leg over fast enough and getting reversed.
2. Not using your weight properly on his chest.

8.15 Mount Reversal: Leg Over

Objective: avoid being mounted and gain a better position.

Immediate danger: being mounted.

Technique:
You are on the bottom of side mount:
- As you face toward your opponent, place your right elbow/forearm against his hip/thigh area.
- Place your left hand under his right arm and above his lat muscle, pointing toward his left shoulder
- Relax
- As he splays his legs and brings a leg over to mount
- Push with your left foot into the mat and point up and over toward his left shoulder with your left arm
- This will reverse the position and will put you in his guard or, side posture if you execute the move early.

Common mistakes:
1. Not setting up in time.
2. Not using your arms/hands properly.
3. Waiting too long to reverse him.

8.16 Mount Reversal: Knee Drag

Objective: to avoid being mounted and gain a better position such as half guard or to full guard.

Immediate danger: being mounted.

Technique:
As he drags his knee across your belly:
- Set up to pull half-guard
- As his knee hits the ground on the opposite side he started from,
- Elbow escape to the back side using your right leg and right elbow, putting him in half guard
- Turn back into your opponent and place your right forearm across his neck to keep him from collapsing on you.
- Brace your left hand against his knee
- Hip out to your right and pull him into full guard.

Common mistakes:
1. Not setting up properly.
2. Waiting too long to perform elbow escape.
3. Allowing him to collapse you in half guard

8.17 Front Choke

Objective: to finish fight with a submission.

Immediate danger: no immediate danger, as you are on the offense.

Technique:
As you have your opponent in your guard:
- Reach across to his opposite collar and place your four fingers into his collar deep, almost all the way behind his neck.
- Reach your other arm across the other way, going UNDER the first arm and placing four fingers deep in the collar on this side.
- Make sure your hands are in very deep, up and around the neck.
- Flex your fists and turn both thumbs toward his ears.
- Pull both of your elbows down toward the mat, expanding your chest, until he taps.

Common mistakes:
1. Not placing your first hand in deep enough.
2. Not placing your second arm UNDER the first.

8.18 Arm Bar from Mount:

Objective: to finish fight with a submission

Immediate danger: losing position

Technique:
As you maintain the mounted position, as the person on the bottom panics and pushes against your chest:
- Select an arm by placing both hands firmly on his chest as he is pushing into your chest as he tries to push you off of him. Your arms will be one inside and one outside the selected arm. (see DVD).
- You have now selected the arm to arm bar: which is the arm you went on the outside of.
- Keep your arms straight and place all of your weight on your hands as you lean forward.
- This takes your body weight off of your legs and onto your hands, pinning your opponent
- As you lean all the way onto him swing your leg around and over his head on the same side as the arm you selected to arm bar.
- As you sit close to his shoulder, keep your knees tight and pull your heels close to his body.
- Secure his wrist with both hands, pointing his thumb toward the ceiling and pinning his wrist to your body.
- Push your hips up toward the ceiling, continuing to pin his arm to your body, finishing the arm bar until he taps.

Common mistakes:
1. Not getting your weight forward.
2. Not selecting an arm.

8.19 Arm Bar from Guard

Objective: to finish fight with a submission.

Immediate danger: opponent passing your guard.

Technique:
As your opponent is in your guard:
- Confirm his right arm behind the elbow with a monkey grip with your right hand.
- Place your left foot in his hip and rotate your body/head to 10 o'clock while AT THE SAME TIME lifting your right leg high into his arm pit and biting down on his back.
- Use your left arm to pull his left shoulder down or pushing his face out of the way as you pass your left leg across his face.
- Keep your knees tight and bring your heels toward your butt locking his arm in place.
- Confirm his wrist to your chest
- Lift your hips up for the submission.

Common mistakes:
1. Not controlling his arm, behind the elbow.
2. Not pivoting your body and using proper leg work.
3. Not confirming wrist to your body.

8.20 Americana a.k.a. Paintbrush

Objective: to finish fight with a submission.

Immediate danger: being rolled, losing position.

As you are mounted on your opponent:
- Reach across with one hand and secure his opposite wrist using a monkey grip and pushing his wrist to the ground using your weight as the leverage. (your right hand, would attack his right arm)
- As you push his arm to the mat, place your forearm on the mat and place your elbow next to his ear.
- Push your free hand under your opponent's triceps and grasp your own wrist, locking everything in tight.
- Maintain your base and pull his arm back toward his hip keeping his hand on the mat as if you are "painting" the mat with his fingers.
- As you pull his arm down toward his hip, begin levering his elbow up with your other arm.
- This will torque his shoulder until he taps to the submission.

Common mistakes:
1. Not keeping the hand secure to the mat.
2. Not locking everything in tight.

8.21 Kimura

Objective: to end fight with submission.

Immediate danger: this is a safe position as you are on the offensive.

As you pull your opponent toward you while he is in your guard, he plants his left hand on the mat near your hip or side:

- Break open your guard and place both feet flat on the mat.
- As you break your guard, reach over with your right hand and control his wrist.
- As you sit up and into your opponent
- Reach over his left shoulder with your left arm
- Reach your left arm, around his left arm and inside his left elbow, grasping your own wrist with a monkey grip.
- Sit back hard toward your left shoulder, while hipping out to the right at the same time.
- Confirm his elbow to your chest and keep his arm bent at a right angle. (90 degrees)
- Hip out a little more and place your right leg across his back, keeping him from rolling.
- Hug his arm tight to your chest and torque his arm toward his head for the submission.

Common mistakes:
1. Not hipping out far enough.
2. Not securing the arm in tight at a 90 degree angle.

8.22: Hip over Sweep

Objective: to gain a better position, mount

Immediate danger: he pushes you back to the mat

- If you try for the Kimura, and he leans forward to bear hug you.
- Stay posted on your right hand, keeping your left arm across his face and over his left shoulder to confirm his arm at his elbow.
- Plant your left foot hard into the mat with your left leg up close to your butt, at about a 90 degree angle.
- Hip up and over toward your right, rolling him over
- As you end up in the mounted position.

Common mistakes:
1. Not confirming his arm at the elbow.
2. Not hipping over hard enough with the legs and hips.
3. Posting on your elbow and not your hand, losing some leverage.

8.23 Guillotine from Guard

Objective: finish the fight with a submission.

Immediate danger: safe position, as you are on the offensive.

- If you are trying for the previous two moves and your opponent leaves his head up and his neck exposed.
- Post on your right arm
- Sit up straight
- Over hook your left arm over and around his neck
- Grab your left wrist with your right hand, locking your arms around his neck.
- Sit back and pull him back into your guard.
- Push your legs out straight as you lift your arms up toward your chin for the submission.

Common mistakes:
1. Not sitting back far enough to create space to get around his neck.
2. Not locking arms around his neck tight enough.

8.24: Guillotine from Standing

Objective: to finish fight with a submission.

Immediate danger: safe position, as you are on the offensive.

- As your opponent comes into you for a takedown, he lowers his head in front of you.
- As he lowers his head, over hook your right arm over and around his neck.
- Grasp your right wrist with your left hand, locking your arms around his neck.
- Turn his head about 3-4 inches in toward your midline and lift slightly as you push your hips forward.
- Tighten as necessary until submission.

Common mistakes:
1. Getting the guillotine, but with one arm in.
2. Not locking your arms around his neck tight enough.
3. Not using the hips to place pressure on his neck.

8.25 Guillotine Defense from Standing

Objective: to survive a choke and eventually gain a better position.

Immediate danger: being choked unconscious.

- In the event you are caught in a guillotine choke from a standing position, you must act quickly and calmly.
- First confirm his wrist, prying your finger inside between his arm and his body.
- As you are confirming his wrist you are dropping in base putting some of your body weight on his choking arm.
- Use your free hand to reach over his same side shoulder with the pleat of your elbow on his shoulder and reaching as far down his back with your hand as you can.
- Place your open hand to the middle of his back.
- This takes the pressure off of your neck and makes you heavy for him.
- Relax and eventually he will tire and let go, setting himself up for the takedown.

Common mistakes:
1. Not protecting the neck quick enough.
2. Not dropping in base.

8.26. Mata Leao:
a.k.a.
The Lion Killer and The Rear Naked Choke

Objective: finish the fight with a submission.

Immediate danger: you are in very a good position on your opponents back with your hooks in. Your main concern is finishing the choke and not allowing your opponent to reverse out of the position.

- As you take your opponents back, put your "hooks" in.
- Place on arm around his neck with your elbow positioned directly under his chin.
- Grasp your opposite bicep with your choking arm
- Bring your other arm behind his head and place it flat on the back of his head.
- Gently lift his head slightly with your arms and squeeze your arms together confirming the choke and the submission.

Common mistakes:

1. Not getting the arm around far enough and under his chin.
2. Not lifting the head slightly before applying pressure.

Technique Rotation:

26 techniques on a four times a year rotation

As you can see we teach the fundamentals of "Kid-Jitsu®" by using 26 of some of the most common and fundamental techniques in Brazilian Jiu-Jitsu. This rotation will take the children through the entire 26 techniques in 13 weeks by doing 2 techniques per week. At the end of the 13 weeks, the techniques will be repeated. You will take your students through this program 4 times in the first year. This will complete "Kid-Jitsu®" Level I for you as a "Kid-Jitsu®" Instructor.

These 26 techniques will coincide with the 26 values that we instill in the Kid-Jitsu® Program. The Kid-Jitsu Values Program* uses one value per week and we stress it repetitively with the children. At one value per week the program is completed after 26 weeks. At that point you will start over and repeat the Values Program which will take you through the program two times in the year.

*NOTE: As a Marital Arts Instructor, you most likely have a character development program in place and you may use this portion of the "Kid-Jitsu®" program as optional.

Once again, the success of a good Brazilian Jiu-Jitsu player is not in how many moves they know, but how many techniques they have perfected. We practice with a lot of repetition of our techniques and we practice them "perfectly."

I do not believe in the old saying that "practice makes perfect." If someone practices the technique but is practicing it wrong, then they will learn to do the technique perfectly wrong!!!

I do however, believe that ***"perfect practice makes perfect."***

Review these notes as you go along with the DVD and commit the techniques to your memory. Also practice them before your classes with your assistants to ensure that you have the confidence and the ability to demonstrate the moves and techniques accurately and "perfectly".

Don't forget: You will be drilling all of these techniques time and time again in your upcoming "Kid-Jitsu®" Instructor Certification Seminar. So do not be overly concerned about your BJJ ability at this point, as you will be drilling these moves to perfection in the very near future. I will not let you leave until you "get it!"…**and you WILL GET IT!**

Also, I cannot stress the importance of viewing the DVD along with the bullet points I've laid out for you in this book. "Mental muscle memory" will begin to take hold the more you saturate you mind with this information. Your physical muscle memory will begin to take hold the more time that you spend on the mat working on and reviewing these 26 techniques.

The key to these techniques as you teach the kids are for YOU to have fun with them. If YOU have fun, the kids will feel the energy coming from you and they will intuitively have fun as well…SO, HAVE FUN!!!

Chapter Nine
The Kid-Jitsu® Values Program

This is where the rubber meets the road in the overall effectiveness of a children's Brazilian Jiu-Jitsu Program. We are in the people business. Sure we are teaching martial arts, but that is just a portion of what we are really teaching. Many parents are entrusting their children to us for several hours per week and it is our responsibility as mature, responsible business owners to take our teaching to a higher level.

We have little human beings, with a fairly blank slate, that we can influence either positively or negatively with every action that we have. They are all eyes and all ears when it comes to what we, as their instructor, are doing.

Credibility in the Values Program: Practice what you preach

The Kid-Jitsu® Values Program covers 26 values that will assist the children in all areas of their lives. It is the backbone of what I wish to accomplish in the entire kids program at my school and also what I wish to share with other schools around the country.

If our Instructors are living it, then they can effectively teach it. If, for example, I am discussing honesty for the week and I have told a fib to one of the students, then my credibility is shot. We must:

Practice what we preach

The Legendary Royce Gracie with Larry and a few of his "Kid-Jitsu®" students at Jacksonville Brazilian Jiu-Jitsu in June 2006

As we teach the Kid-Jitsu Values Program we are giving the children a framework for their decision making process that will be with them for the rest of their lives. If their parents spend a lot of time with them, then most likely we are just reaffirming what their parents are teaching them. If they are not getting much time from their parents, our values program will be the lynch pin for their character development. I am totally dedicated to Brazilian Jiu-Jitsu, but I am absolutely "sold out" to this portion of the Kid-Jitsu Program. As Coaches in the Kid-Jitsu® Values Program we must:

- Sit down with the kids in each class and get "on their level" with the value of the week.
- As questions like: "Who can tell me what honesty is?"

- Get class participation: "Give me an example of when you were honest when you thought telling the truth would get you in trouble?"
- "Can you tell me a time when you were not honest?" "How did that make you feel?"
- Given another opportunity, would you do things differently next time?"
- Follow up every class for the week using the same value.
- Get accountability from the students. "Give me an example of how you were honest in a situation since I saw you on Tuesday."

The Kid-Jitsu® Values Program

The Kid-Jitsu Values program covers one value per week for 26 weeks. At the end of the 26 weeks you will start over at #1. Where you cover the "Kid-Jitsu®" Fundamentals 4 times per year, you will cover the "Kid-Jitsu®" Values Program 2 times per year.

Here is a listing of the 26 Values that we cover over and over in the "Kid-Jitsu®" Values Program.

1. Honesty: telling the truth always!
2. Integrity: do what you say you will do when you say you'll do it.
3. Self-Esteem: loving yourself in a healthy way, you are your own best friend.
4. Self-Motivation: encouraging yourself to do what you need to do in school, "Kid-Jitsu®", at home, in extracurricular activities.
5. Self-Image: how you view yourself and how you talk to yourself.
6. Self-Respect: valuing yourself, treat your body like a temple; feed your mind "good stuff."
7. Trust: Belief in others.
8. Faithfulness: believe in things you cannot see. (fruit of the spirit)
9. Goodness: being "good" in all that you do. "Do the right thing!" (fruit of the spirit)
10. Character: your character is who you are, when no one is around.
11. Reliability: being there and being willing to assist others.
12. Kindness: treating others nice, and the way YOU like to be treated, "The Golden Rule".

13. Perseverance: continue working toward a goal even when you want to quit!
14. Humor: having fun but NOT making fun of others.
15. Self-Awareness: knowing yourself and how your actions affect others.
16. Respect for others: valuing others and showing them the value you place on them.
17. Listening Skills: hearing is not just listening.
18. Self-Control: control your mind and control your actions. You are **responsible** for being in control of your mind and your actions!
19. Self-Discipline: doing what you **NEED** to do, not what you **WANT** to do.
20. Positive Attitude: looking at the "bright side", what is the bright side?
21. Sharing: having a giving heart.
22. Joy: loving life! (fruit of the spirit)
23. Love: there are different types of love. (fruit of the spirit)
24. Patience: remain calm, not in a hurry. It is not just waiting, but what YOU DO while you wait. (fruit of the spirit)
25. Gentleness: being "gentle" in all that you do.
26. Peace: feeling of well being. (fruit of the spirit)

Chapter Ten
What Makes a Good "Kid-Jitsu® Program?"

"It's Showtime...who is running the show?"

My Kid-Jitsu® classes begin the moment the children walk in the door of the Academy. They are asked to sign themselves in (as well as they can, given their age), bow onto the mat and have a seat in the middle of the mat. My "Kid-Jitsu®" students are required to "take responsibility" as soon as they walk in the door and sign in.

As the other kids begin to arrive, they all do the same thing; sign in, bow onto the mat and have a seat in the middle of the mat. Eventually they all end up in the center of the mat, in one group and they are having casual conversation. We are very aware of the interactions of the children and I will squash a clique in a skinny minute.

Why will I not allow cliques? My concern is for the well being and confidence of **every child** in my care for that hour. I will not allow any child to be ostracized from the group. All of these kids are created equally and there is no favoritism from me, my Instructors and there are absolutely no "cliques" in my school.

As the group begins to grow, I have a seat in the group with them and I begin to connect with them, on their level. We talk about just about everything, video games, movies, what happened in school, family, pets, you name it! The key is to get into their world, learn a little more about them and what some of their interests are.

Listen to what they have to say and you can connect with them better and better as more classes go by.

When it is time to begin class, I call for them to line up. Upper level belts first, followed by lower ranks. If there is a visitor in class, I sign an upper level belt to be their "mentor" for that class and they line up with their mentor.

Line up and Pledge to the flag

I select a "leader" for each class at this time. The leader begins and leads the pledge to the flag. Upon completion of the pledge, we discuss what the flag means and why we pledge allegiance to the flag.

"Does anyone know why we pledge the flag?"

I take and briefly discuss a few of their answers and then we move on to doing our stretches, warm-up and cardio exercises.

Warm-ups and body weight exercises

Our warm-up is fairly standard including:

- Stretches from head to toe
- Crunches
- Push ups
- Hindu Squats
- Planks
- And many more options, with all exercises being age appropriate.

Cardiovascular drills:

The cardiovascular drills are done around the perimeter of our mat. The key is to get the kids heart rate up. I use this time as a time to ENCOURAGE every child in some way: "Way to work Andrew!!", "Great Job Ally!!", "Nice job finishing strong Austin!!", "You guys are awesome."

Every child needs encouragement and here and through the end of class we hand it out in VERY LARGE DOSES!

A few of the drills that we do to work the body and get their heart rate up are:

- Front rolls.
- Frog hops
- Bear crawls
- Army crawls
- Baby crawls
- Crab crawls
- Duck walks
- Shrimp Drills
- Sprawls
- Races: doing the above mentioned drills.

They LOVE the races and it's a great warm-up for the Jiu-Jitsu techniques that they will be practicing. Relay races with team names: split the class up, pick a leader, and let them come up with a name. Let the leader get everything organized and let them have a ball. Encourage them to also encourage their team mates.

"Kid-Jitsu®" Value of the week:

After we complete the warm-up and cardio drills, I gather everyone over to the edge of the mat where I have a dry erase board.

At this time I write the value of the week on the board and begin asking questions:

Using Honesty as an example, here are the types of questions I would ask to engage them:

- "Who can tell me what honesty is?"
- "How would you demonstrate being honest?"
- "Have you ever been dishonest?"
- "How did that make you feel?"
- "What would you do differently if you faced this situation again?"
- "What lesson did you learn?"

Through the various questions, I ascertain that the children:
- Understand the value being discussed.
- Can give me an example of how this value is used in everyday life.
- Understand and can communicate right from wrong.
- Use the value throughout the week.

Select the Value of the week and stick to it for that given week. They are put in order from 1-26 and I recommend that you stay in order to keep things on track for the long haul. I've found that if I try to "skip" around, I will eventually skip one or two of the values in the rotation, and I don't want to miss any of them with my kids.

Technique:

As we move from the Value of the week to the technique we play a little game of "Mr. Larry says". Kids of all ages LOVE this game:

Mr. Larry says "stand in base."
Right arm up---got you Jimmy, go have a seat.
Mr. Larry says take 3 steps forward, etc..

Once we have a winner (or several winners-as they can be tough to trick) I have them all line up on the edge of the mat.

I have an Assistant Instructor come onto the mat with me and I demonstrate the technique we are going to cover for the class. I demonstrate it 4-5 times and then we split them up and have them practice the technique at least 10 times each.

As the children are working on the technique, me and my assistants walk around and work individually with the various students. The kids get a lot from the one on one instruction during this time from me and my assistants.

After many repetitions and one on one "tightening up" of their technique, we will come back to the edge of the mat and we will discuss the technique, I will have them "talk me through" the technique, very similar to the bullet points I have provided for you.

By doing this:

- They have seen the technique.
- They have performed the technique.
- They have thought through and verbalized the technique.

We have hit many of their senses and they "get it" quicker than you and I ever could at this point in our careers.

In every class I emphasize the importance of repetition and developing muscle memory. The more we do it, the better we get. They know it, and they embrace it, and they are getting pretty darn good in Brazilian Jiu-Jitsu.

Trouble shooting

All of the children may not "get it" on the first rotation, but we will review it the next class. By the end of the week they will see it and practice it again at least once more. We will touch on these techniques in review the following week and we will "coach" them to use the techniques they have seen every time in sparring.

Sparring

Sparring is, without a doubt, the most exciting part of the class for the kids. They LOVE to spar. A few quick thoughts on how to let them spar:

- Start them from their knees about 90% of the time. I do this to keep the injuries to a minimum.
- Have them shake hands before and after the sparring session.
- Have them spar 1-2 minutes. If any of my kids participate in tournaments, I will prepare them by doing 4 minute rounds.
- Always pair them up with a person their size, age and ability.
- Keep an eye on everyone you pair up.
- One adult or coach per one pair sparring.
- Verbally tap for them 'loudly' when they are even close to being submitted with a choke or arm bar or shoulder lock.
- Raise "both" of their arms as winners at the end of sparring.
- Verbally acknowledge that they did a "good job" and call them by their names. "Great Job Kellen, Awesome work Adrienne!"

Line Up to End the Class

As the sparring ends and all of the children have gotten their "reps" in sparring, I call everybody up to line up. They line up in the same order that they lined up in to start the class.

This is the time that I make announcements to the class, give single stripe promotions, discuss the technique that we learned that day and also briefly remind them of the value of the week.

We end the class with two things:

- We read/recite the "Kid-Jitsu®" Creed.
- As they are lined up I say: "We end every class with…"
- We all say together: "RESPECT"

Each child then files in behind the leader and they all pass by the instructors and shake hands. Each child is expected to look you in the eyes and shake your right hand with their right hand. The instructors say "good job" and they must say "thank you" as they look you in the eyes.

Chapter Eleven
What Makes a Good Kid-Jitsu® Instructor?

A good Kid-Jitsu® Instructor has many qualities. However there are **five** areas that I feel must be implemented into the school itself for one to be successful and there are also **seven qualities** that one must have if they are going to be a successful instructor.

The five "must haves" for the successful school:

A successful Kid-Jitsu® Program must have the following elements ingrained into their system:

- Structure
- Respect
- Fun
- Repetition
- Consistency and Predictability

Structure: Having had children of my own, I found out over time that kids LOVE structure. They will always test the limits that you set in the structure, but with some good "one minute management" and being "consistent and predictable" with the discipline, they will fall in line with the structure that a responsible adult puts before them.

Please note: I am not saying that it will be easy with every child, because it's not. However I do feel that a structure coupled with accountability and consistency in discipline typically works with most children.

Respect: Respect has got to be a mutual deal. How can I expect ANYONE to respect me if I am disrespectful to ANYONE? As the leader in the school, I make it a point to show the utmost respect for all of my students; children and adults, my assistants, the parents and any visitors who visit the school. Respect comes back to me at least ten-fold.

Fun: Have fun. Be fun. Make it fun for everyone. This one's easy! We are doing what we love to do, making a good living, staying in great shape…playing with the kids.

Consistency and Predictability: We've covered this. Tape this one to your mirror or your computer monitor. If you have any problems with managing people, remember these two words and implement what I have said into your management game. You will be glad that you did.

Repetition: Do it now, do it right, then do it again and again and again and again…

Remember:

"Practice does not make perfect…perfect practice makes perfect."

The Seven "must haves" for the successful Kid-Jitsu® Instructor

A successful Kid-Jitsu® Instructor must have and demonstrate the following traits:

Personality
Respectable and Respectful
Structured
Disciplined
Knowledgeable
Consistent and Predictable
You've got to love them like your own.

Personality: This is the charge that sets the fire in the class and on the mats. Again have fun, be "up" for the kids, use your humor in the class.

Some people have it and some people have to work at it. If you have trouble connecting with people, consider taking a Tony Robbins type of course. I went through many of these types of programs in my "first" career and you can always gain something from these programs when you are striving for self improvement.

Respectable and Respectful: As the Main Instructor in my Academy, I have got to be a respectable person and I must be respectful of everyone I come in contact with.

How can I ask this of others, if I don't ask it of myself? Quite Simply, I can't!

Structured: I covered this above in the qualities of a successful school. You've got to have your game together in every area.

Disciplined: Expect the same from yourself that you expect of your students. If you are preaching the benefits of good health and exercise, yet you are 30 lbs overweight, you are lacking the discipline that you are asking your students to have. We all must, again, practice what we preach.

Knowledgeable: Know this information backward, forward and inside out. There are 26 techniques and you have it on video and in this manual. Commit yourself to being the "Kid-Jitsu®" expert in your city. Knowledge and practice brings confidence, and it's tough to discourage a confident man or woman.

Consistent and Predictable: You've got to commit to this school management style!

Love them like your own: We can have a tremendous impact in these children's lives and that's an awesome responsibility. I love 'em, and I know you do too!

Conclusion

"Kid-Jitsu®" is a Brazilian Jiu-Jitsu based children's martial arts program. The intent of this publication has been to assist the traditional martial arts Instructor in adding a ground based program into their current system.

The techniques in the system are technically correct and fundamentally sound. With proper technique and repetition the "Kid-Jitsu®" Instructor and the student can master the fundamentals of "Kid-Jitsu®" and in the long term-Brazilian Jiu-Jitsu.

The study of martial arts is a marathon, not a sprint. The organization of the "Kid-Jitsu®" Program, Volume One is at the very foundation for all Martial Arts Instructors and their child students to begin to develop a superior foundation of Brazilian Jiu-Jitsu.

The one on one, "live" sparring sessions, with submissions, will give the children a sense of being able to defend their selves, while attaining a sense of accomplishment and confidence that cannot be duplicated.

Glossary of "Kid-Jitsu®" Terms

Americana: the Americana is the name of a bent arm lock that is also referred to as the "paintbrush".

Arm bar: the arm bar is a technique used to straighten an opponents arm to put undue stress on the elbow joint.

Bug the neck: this is a term I use to remind my students to always work on the choke to open up other attacks.

Base: the proper balance and proper use of your body weight.

Choke: a variety of techniques to cut off blood flow through the carotid arteries to the brain. This can cause the opponent to "pass out" and must be practiced with extreme care and safety.

Elbow Escape: a technique that uses hip and leg leverage to place one's opponent back in their guard.

Gi: the kimono or uniform used in Brazilian Jiu-Jitsu

Guard: a position where one is lying on their back and has their legs wrapped around their opponent who is in front of them and on their knees.

Guillotine: a choke that uses the forearm/arm to choke their opponent.

Hip out: a technique used to create space between you and your opponent.

"Kid-Jitsu®": the trademarked registered Program that teaches Brazilian Jiu-Jitsu to children.

"Kid-Jitsu®" Values Program: the values program that is aligned with "Kid-Jitsu®"

Kimura: a bent arm lock that puts immense amount of stress on the shoulder socket. Named after the famed Japanese Judo Champion: Kimura.

Lapel: the collar of the Gi.

Leverage: in this instance will be the use of your body control and angles without using your physical strength, to be able to move your opponent to a position you wish to put him in. Leverage is not power!

Monkey grip: grabbing your opponent in such a manner that you thumb and four fingers are on the same side.

Mount: straddling ones opponent when they are flat on their back.

Osoto Gari: a takedown using, the opponents Gi and your own footwork, base and leverage to take your opponent to the ground.

Overhook: wrapping your arm up and around your opponents arm.

Paintbrush: see Americana.

Pass the Guard: Moving around/past your opponents legs as you gain a better position.

Post or Post up: placing your foot or hand on the ground to keep your balance, and not lose position.

Posture: utilize the balance and weight of your body not to be thrown off balance by your opponent.

Side Posture, Side Control: chest to chest with your opponent with you legs out and perpendicular to your opponent's legs.

Shrimp: see hipping out.

Spar or Sparring: a timed session of grappling that allows the student to practice their skills in a live setting.

Submission: to make one's opponent want to quit due to some form of arm lock, choke or other joint lock.

Sweep: to reverse the position.

Take Down: take one's opponent to the ground.

Tap Out: to submit to your opponent by "tapping" him to let him know you wish to stop.

Thumb in: when reaching for ones collar up by his neck, the thumb will be placed inside the collar and the four fingers out.

Thumb out: when reaching for ones collar up by his neck, the 4 fingers will be placed inside the collar and the thumb will be out.

Underhook: hook your arm between your opponents arm and his body.

Upa: a move used with your hip and legs to reverse your opponents.

"Kid-Jitsu®" Licensing

Would you like to easily implement "Kid-Jitsu®" into your school? Review the attached:

Authorized Kid-Jitsu® Program

"Kid-Jitsu®" Licensed teaching authorization is available to appropriately experienced school owners and instructors in their schools. There are many benefits to teaching the "Kid-Jitsu®" program at your school including:

- Marketing your school with the use of the Certified "Kid-Jitsu®" credentials.
- A top notch ground fighting program for children.
- Increased child enrollment.
- Improved child retention.
- Improved family enrollment.
- Additional upgrade and revenue opportunities.
- Enhancement and/or reaffirmation of your market position.

"Kid-Jitsu®" provides unparalleled support including:
Comprehensive Instructor Certification, detailed curriculum guides
and training manuals for Instructor and students;
comprehensive Instructor and student training DVD's; periodic local and
regional single and multi-day intensive seminars; yearly technical
materials upgrade up to 4 stripe Green Belt.

For more information call:

The International Kid-Jitsu Association Headquarters (I.K.J.A.)
at:

904-242-9343.

Or visit

www.kid-jitsu.net
or
www.jaxbjj.com

Afterword

About Jacksonville Brazilian Jiu-Jitsu a.k.a. JaxBJJ

The Jacksonville Brazilian Jiu-Jitsu Academy is a Royce Gracie Affiliate and is located in Neptune Beach, Florida. The school currently has just over 200 students in our program which includes Kid-Jitsu®, Gracie Jiu-Jitsu, Haganah F.I.G.H.T. , Haganah F.I.T., and Muay Thai.

Just 1 mile from the beach, the Jacksonville Brazilian Jiu-Jitsu Academy is the location where the "Kid-Jitsu®" Instructor Certification's will be completed. Come join us in the fastest growing and most efficient "upgrade" that your school could possibly have.

For more information about Kid-Jitsu® and/or Jacksonville Brazilian Jiu-Jitsu please go to:

www.kid-jitsu.net
www.jaxbjj.com

Acknowledgements

I wish to express my gratitude and sincere thanks to the following people:

I wish to thank Royce Gracie for being my Instructor and friend. I'd like to thank my wife Gail for encouraging me to leave the headaches of the corporate world behind so I could pursue what I have a passion for doing, and that is to teach children and adult's Royce Gracie Jiu-Jitsu, Kid-Jitsu®, Haganah F.I.G.H.T. and F.I.T. and Muay Thai.

Thanks also to all of my students at JaxBJJ for their hard work and belief in the program. Thank you to the children and parents of the original "Kid-Jitsu®" program. And last but not least, I wish to thank the "Leadership Team" at JaxBJJ for all that they have done and continue to do to make JaxBJJ a great place to train.

The Leadership Team is a band of extraordinary folks with many varied talents, a ton of dedication, some funky names and even funkier personalities. Guys like Zamarillo, Jimmy G., Irish, Dirty Dean, Reverend Joby, Phil, Dilly, Doc, Kohl, T.J., Brendo your Frendo, Old Rob, Nate a.k.a. Big Dumb Guy, and our Art Director and Webmaster extraordinaire: Chris Debelen--you guys are awesome and are truly what makes JaxBJJ such a great place to train for all of our students. Thanks!!

Larry Shealy
August, 2006

Printed in the United States
65487LVS00003B/314